CRANES

by Aubrey Zalewski

Cody Koala

An Imprint of Pop!
popbooksonline.com

abdobooks.com

Published by Pop!, a division of ABDO, PO Box 398166, Minneapolis, Minnesota 55439. Copyright © 2020 by POP, LLC. International copyrights reserved in all countries. No part of this book may be reproduced in any form without written permission from the publisher. Pop!™ is a trademark and logo of POP, LLC.

Printed in the United States of America, North Mankato, Minnesota

052019
092019

♻ THIS BOOK CONTAINS RECYCLED MATERIALS

Cover Photo: iStockphoto
Interior Photos: iStockphoto, 1, 5, 7 (top), 7 (bottom left), 7 (bottom right), 9, 10, 13, 15, 17, 18, 20, 21

Editor: Meg Gaertner
Series Designer: Sophie Geister-Jones

Library of Congress Control Number: 2018964593

Publisher's Cataloging-in-Publication Data

Names: Zalewski, Aubrey, author.
Title: Cranes / by Aubrey Zalewski.
Description: Minneapolis, Minnesota : Pop!, 2020 | Series: Construction vehicles | Includes online resources and index.
Identifiers: ISBN 9781532163302 (lib. bdg.) | ISBN 9781644940037 (pbk.) |ISBN 9781532164743 (ebook)
Subjects: LCSH: Cranes, derrick, etc.--Juvenile literature. | Construction equipment--Juvenile literature. | Construction industry--Equipment and supplies--Juvenile literature.
Classification: DDC 621.8--dc23

Hello! My name is
Cody Koala

Pop open this book and you'll find QR codes like this one, loaded with information, so you can learn even more!

Scan this code* and others like it while you read, or visit the website below to make this book pop.

popbooksonline.com/cranes

*Scanning QR codes requires a web-enabled smart device with a QR code reader app and a camera.

Table of Contents

The Crane Can Help!

Construction workers are building a mall. They need to move a beam to the top floor. A crane lifts the beam high. It puts the beam into place.

Watch a video here!

A Crane's Job

Cranes carry **loads**. They lift large objects to high places. They move heavy objects short distances.

Some cranes can lift the weight of 15 school buses!

Complete an activity here!

Chapter 3

Parts of a Boom Crane

A **boom** crane is a construction vehicle. It has many parts. The boom is a long arm. It sticks out from the crane's base. It moves the **load**.

Learn more here!

The **jib** connects to the boom. It makes the boom longer. It lets the boom reach farther.

The boom can turn in different directions.

Cranes lift things using **pulleys**. Strong rope attaches to the load. The rope curves around a wheel at the crane's top. The crane pulls the rope down on one side of the wheel. This lifts the load up on the other side.

ropes pulled down

load lifted up

load

Loads are heavy. Cranes can tip over when lifting them. To prevent this, cranes have **counterweights**. The weights help hold the crane down.

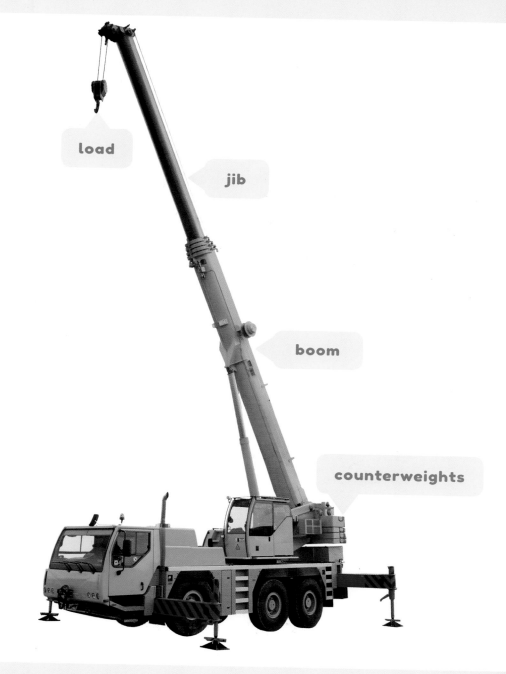

load

jib

boom

counterweights

Chapter 4

Types of Cranes

Many **boom** cranes move on wheels. Other cranes stay in one place. Tower cranes are very tall. They help build **skyscrapers**.

Learn more here!

Bridge cranes also stay in one place. They are often built into the roofs of buildings. Bridge cranes move things from side to side.

Some cranes are on ships.

They help build bridges.

Some cranes float
on water.

Other cranes go on the backs of trucks. These cranes have booms that can grow and shrink.

Making Connections

Text-to-Self

Have you ever seen a crane at work? What was it doing? What kind of crane was it?

Text-to-Text

Have you read about another construction machine? How is its job similar to a crane's? How is it different?

Text-to-World

A crane has many parts that work together. What are other machines that have many parts? What would happen if one of the parts stopped working?

Glossary

boom – a long arm that sticks out from a crane's base.

counterweight – a heavy weight used to balance a load and keep a crane from falling over.

jib – an arm that connects to the boom and helps the boom reach farther.

load – a large or heavy object that is being carried.

pulley – a simple machine that uses ropes and wheels to make lifting easier.

skyscraper – a very tall building.

Index

Online Resources

popbooksonline.com

Thanks for reading this Cody Koala book!

Scan this code* and others like it in this book, or visit the website below to make this book pop!

popbooksonline.com/cranes

*Scanning QR codes requires a web-enabled smart device with a QR code reader app and a camera.